The Mediator

The Art of Mediation: Techniques, Case Studies and Insights

Geo Report
2023

Chapter 1: Introduction to Mediation

We enter the intriguing territory of mediation, a form of conflict resolution that stands out for its effectiveness and humanized approach. Far from the traditional trails that often lead to long and exhausting legal processes, mediation offers an agile and respectful way to resolve disputes.

At the core of mediation, we find the ability to build bridges between disagreeing parties, seeking a common understanding. It's like a delicate dance of conversations that unfolds, led by a skilled mediator, with the aim of reaching fair and lasting agreements.

In this chapter, we will delve into the basics of mediation, exploring its nuances and understanding why it stands out as an intelligent alternative in our search for harmony in relationships. Mediation is not limited to resolving disputes; it preserves dignity, protects privacy, and keeps the door open for ongoing dialogue.

As we move forward on this journey, prepare to discover the techniques, skills and insights that make mediation an essential tool for achieving mutual understanding, equity and, above all, for building more solid and peaceful relationships.

- What is mediation and its importance in conflict resolution

Mediation is a notable approach to conflict resolution. Think of it as a kind of "guided conversation" between the parties in disagreement, under the guidance of an impartial and skilled mediator. Rather than facing escalating disputes or protracted court proceedings, mediation seeks collaboration and mutual understanding.

Its importance lies in the fact that it offers a faster, more economical and humane way to solve differences. It excels at preserving relationships, allowing parties to express their concerns and aspirations in a respectful manner, while working together to find common ground.

The key here is to prevent conflicts from deepening into insurmountable antagonisms. Instead, mediation encourages empathy, dialogue and the search for constructive solutions. It is a tool that transcends individual disputes, offering a means to maintain the dignity, privacy and integrity of the parties involved.

Mediation, therefore, not only resolves issues effectively, but also lays the groundwork for future healthier interactions and for building lasting relationships. It's a wise and compassionate choice, demonstrating that understanding can prevail even in the most tense of situations.

- Advantages and benefits of using mediation

The adoption of mediation offers a number of substantial advantages and notable benefits. These attributes make it a powerful and highly effective instrument in conflict resolution, standing out among conventional alternatives.

First, mediation is a shorter road to dispute resolution. By avoiding lengthy and complex court proceedings, it saves valuable time for all parties involved. This is especially crucial in a world where the pace of modern life is dizzying.

In addition, mediation has a positive economic impact. It reduces the considerable costs associated with legal litigation, alleviating the financial burden that often accompanies the pursuit of justice. This resource savings can be significant, allowing parties to direct their efforts and resources to other important areas of their lives.

However, perhaps the most valuable benefit of mediation is its ability to preserve relationships. Unlike court battles, which often leave a trail of bitterness and resentment, mediation fosters an environment where mutual understanding can flourish. This is particularly important in scenarios involving family, business or communities, where maintaining ties is essential.

Privacy is another gem in the mediation arsenal. By keeping the issues under discussion out of public view, it preserves dignity and avoids unpleasant exposure. This can be crucial to avoid embarrassment and to protect the reputation of the parties involved.

Finally, mediation is a platform that allows the parties to be protagonists of their own resolution. They have an active voice in building the agreement, which often results in more lasting and satisfactory solutions. This direct participation is a powerful asset, as the parties feel heard and invested in the process.

The advantages and benefits of mediation are considerable. It provides a faster, more economical and constructive way to resolve conflicts, preserving relationships, privacy and allowing the parties to be protagonists in the search for fair and sustainable solutions.

- How mediation differs from other dispute resolution methods

The distinction between mediation and other methods of conflict resolution is a crucial aspect to be explored. This essential difference lies in the approach, the results achieved and the dynamics of the interactions involved.

Unlike court disputes, where a judge is tasked with making binding decisions, mediation involves an impartial third party, the mediator. The mediator acts as a guide, facilitating communication between the conflicting parties. Instead of dictating a verdict, it encourages the search for consensus, allowing the parties to be the creators of their own solution.

This is one of the most striking distinctions: Mediation empowers the parties to actively participate in creating the agreement, giving them a sense of control and responsibility. This direct involvement often results in more lasting and satisfying solutions, as both parties feel heard and invested in the outcome.

Furthermore, mediation is highly confidential. Unlike court proceedings that often expose sensitive issues to the public, mediation preserves the privacy of the parties. This is especially crucial in situations where discretion is paramount, such as family disputes, business disputes or confidentiality issues.

Another important distinction is the constructive atmosphere of the mediation. While court proceedings tend to accentuate conflict and the polarization of parties, mediation seeks to establish a platform where dialogue and understanding can flourish. This is especially valuable when it comes to maintaining ongoing relationships, such as in family situations or business disputes.

Mediation differs from other conflict resolution methods for its collaborative approach, the direct involvement of the parties, the confidentiality it preserves and the constructive atmosphere it promotes. These elements combined make mediation a valuable choice for those seeking solutions that go beyond the unilateral decision and that preserve the dignity and relationships involved.

Chapter 2: Fundamentals of Mediation

At the heart of mediation lie the foundations that underpin this unique and effective approach to conflict resolution. We'll explore these essential pillars, understanding the foundations on which mediation rests, the skills a skilled mediator must possess, and the importance of sound ethical principles.

Mediation is more than just a technique; It is a specialized form of communication. This requires exceptional interpersonal skills from the mediator. The ability to listen actively, to understand the nuances of the emotions at play, and to communicate clearly and respectfully are crucial attributes.

A mediator must be neutral, impartial and free from conflicts of interest. The parties' confidence in their neutrality is essential to the success of the process. In addition, the mediator must be able to control the dynamics of the conversations, ensuring that the discussions move forward in a constructive manner, without either party feeling disadvantaged.

Another key point is the ethical principles that guide the work of the mediator. Confidentiality is a central pillar; information shared during mediation must be protected at all costs. The mediator must also promote a safe environment where all parties feel respected and heard.

In addition, the mediator's competence also includes the ability to identify the appropriate moments to intervene. This entails knowing when to ask direct questions, when to suggest solutions, and when to simply allow parties to explore their own perspectives.

By understanding these fundamentals, we will be ready to appreciate the crucial role the mediator plays in the mediation process. A skilled mediator is essential to create an environment that favors communication, mutual understanding and, ultimately, the construction of solutions that reflect the interests and needs of the parties involved.

- Ethical principles and skills of the mediator

The ethical principles and skills of a mediator form the solid foundation on which mediation rests. These fundamentals are essential for conducting a fair, respectful and effective process that promotes understanding and the search for collaborative solutions.

The impartiality of the mediator is at the heart of these principles. He should be a neutral guide, free of personal interests and prejudices, ensuring that the parties involved feel equally heard and valued. Confidence in the neutrality of the mediator is fundamental for the process to work properly.

In addition, confidentiality is an essential pillar. The mediator must ensure that all information shared during mediation sessions is kept strictly confidential. This creates a safe environment where parties can express their concerns and interests without fear of public exposure.

The mediator's competence encompasses a diverse range of skills. The ability to listen actively is crucial. It is through this careful listening that the mediator understands the perspectives of each party, identifying their underlying interests and needs.

Clear communication is another key competence. The mediator must convey information in an accessible and respectful manner, avoiding legal jargon or confusing language. This clarity facilitates mutual understanding and contributes to the development of workable solutions.

The ability to control the process is also critical. The mediator must ensure that conversations move forward in a productive manner, avoiding tangents that do not lead to the desired agreement. At the same time, it must allow the parties to have a voice, exploring their points of view and seeking common ground.

Ethical interaction and the mediator's skills are a foundation that allows mediation to be effective, constructive and respectful. It is this balance between neutrality, confidentiality and communication skills that makes mediation such a valuable tool for conflict resolution, allowing parties to find common ground and work together towards mutually satisfactory solutions.

- Essential communication skills for an effective mediator

Communication skills play a crucial role in a mediator's effectiveness. It is these skills that allow the mediator to create an environment conducive to mutual understanding, dialogue and, finally, the construction of collaborative solutions.

The first of these skills is active listening. The mediator must listen carefully, not just to the words, but also to the underlying emotions and feelings of the parties involved. Through this careful listening, the mediator understands each other's perspectives, identifying interests and concerns.

Empathy is another key skill. It allows the mediator to put himself in the shoes of the parties, understanding their experiences and feelings. Empathy creates a human connection, building trust and demonstrating to parties that their points of view are valued.

Clear communication is essential. The mediator must be able to convey information in an accessible and concise manner, avoiding technical or ambiguous language. This is especially important when it comes to helping parties understand the available options and possible outcomes.

The ability to ask open-ended questions is a powerful asset. Questions that encourage parties to explore their own perspectives, interests, and solutions create an environment of self-discovery, leading to more lasting and satisfying solutions.

Finally, conflict management is a skill that the mediator must possess. Conflicts can arise during sessions, and the mediator must be able to deal with them calmly, constructively and impartially, ensuring that communication does not disintegrate, but moves towards resolution.

These communication skills are the essence of the effective mediator. They allow the mediator to act as a skilled facilitator, creating a space where parties can express themselves, understand each other, and ultimately reach a mutually satisfactory agreement.

- The role of the mediator in the mediation process

The mediator plays a central and distinctive role in the mediation process. Its presence is essential to create an environment conducive to constructive conflict resolution, where the parties involved can collaborate and seek mutually satisfactory solutions.

First, the mediator is an impartial facilitator. Your neutrality is key to ensuring that the process is fair and that all parties feel heard and respected. This neutrality lends credibility to the process and allows parties to trust that their perspective will be considered.

In addition, the mediator is a skilled communicator. He must be able to actively listen, understand the concerns and interests of the parties, and convey information in a clear and accessible manner. Such effective communication is essential for parties to understand the available options and to be able to make informed decisions.

The mediator is also a guide in the conflict resolution process. It helps parties explore their views, identify areas of agreement, and work together to find solutions. The mediator does not dictate the outcome, but instead encourages the parties to be the creators of their own solution.

In addition, the mediator can strategically intervene to prevent communication from deviating or becoming unproductive. He can ask thought-provoking questions, suggest alternatives, and help keep the focus on reaching an agreement.

Finally, the mediator is a guardian of the confidentiality and integrity of the process. It ensures that information shared during mediation sessions is kept confidential and that all parties are treated with respect and fairness.

The mediator plays a multifaceted role in the mediation process. Their neutrality, communication skills, guidance and process management are essential to create an environment conducive to constructive conflict resolution, allowing the parties to collaborate and seek solutions that reflect their interests and needs.

Chapter 3: Preparing for Mediation

In the third chapter, we dive into the crucial step of preparing for mediation. This phase is essential to ensure that the process is productive and effective, providing an environment conducive to constructive conflict resolution.

Preparation begins with choosing the right mediator. It is crucial to select someone with the interpersonal skills, neutrality and knowledge necessary to facilitate the mediation process impartially and effectively.

In addition, the parties involved must be prepared for mediation. This includes gathering all relevant information about the conflict, identifying your goals and interests, and being willing to actively participate in the process.

Preparation also involves creating a suitable physical and emotional environment for mediation. Sessions should take place in a quiet, private location where parties feel comfortable expressing their concerns and perspectives.

Clear communication is a key part of preparation. Parties should be aware that mediation is an opportunity to express themselves and listen to each other in a respectful manner. This requires a willingness to listen actively and an open mind to understand other parties' points of view.

Also, it's important to set realistic expectations. Mediation may not resolve all conflicts perfectly, but it does provide an opportunity to find mutually acceptable solutions. The parties must be willing to compromise on some points and work together to find common ground.

Preparing for mediation is a key step that lays the groundwork for a successful mediation process. When all parties are properly prepared, the environment is ripe for constructive communication, collaboration and, ultimately, the search for solutions that meet the interests and needs of all involved.

- Identification of conflicts suitable for mediation

Identifying conflicts suitable for mediation is a crucial step in ensuring that this approach is effective and successful. Not all conflicts are appropriate for mediation, and understanding which situations benefit most from this approach is essential.

First, conflicts involving ongoing issues and relationships that need to be preserved are excellent candidates for mediation. If the parties have a mutual interest in maintaining a relationship, be it personal or professional, mediation can be a valuable tool for finding common ground and restoring harmony.

Furthermore, conflicts where privacy and confidentiality are important are often suitable for mediation. Mediation sessions are confidential, allowing parties to discuss sensitive issues without fear of public exposure. This is especially relevant in cases of family disputes, business confidentiality issues or other sensitive matters.

Complex conflicts involving technical or legal issues can also benefit from mediation. The mediator often has expertise in relevant areas, which helps to ensure that the parties understand all the implications and possible solutions.

However, it is important to recognize that not all conflicts are suitable for mediation. In situations where there is abuse, extreme power imbalance, or an unwillingness on one side to participate in good faith, other approaches may be more appropriate.

Identifying conflicts suitable for mediation is an essential part of the process. It ensures that mediation is targeted to the scenarios where it can make the most difference, allowing parties to collaborate constructively to find solutions that meet their interests and needs, while preserving relationships and privacy where necessary.

- Establishment of an environment conducive to mediation

Establishing an enabling environment is a vital element in the mediation process. This environment is critical to promoting effective communication, empathy and, ultimately, allowing the parties involved to collaborate in the search for constructive solutions.

It starts with choosing a suitable location for mediation sessions. This space should be quiet, private, and comfortable, creating an environment where parties feel comfortable expressing their thoughts and concerns without distractions or interruptions.

The physical layout of the chairs is also important. A circular or semi-circular arrangement of chairs can be more supportive than a confrontational arrangement, helping to create a sense of equality and allowing parties to see and communicate directly.

In addition, the mediator plays a key role in creating the right environment. Your neutrality, empathy and communication skills are essential in establishing an atmosphere of respect and openness. It should make the parties feel heard and valued, creating a solid foundation for dialogue.

Confidentiality is also an integral part of this enabling environment. Parties must feel that their conversations are confidential, allowing them to share sensitive information without fear of public exposure. This is key to allowing the underlying issues to be candidly explored.

The mindset of the parties is also relevant. They must be willing to actively participate in the process, actively listening, respecting others' perspectives, and seeking collaborative solutions. The mindset of finding common ground and seeking solutions rather than unilateral victory is crucial.

Establishing an enabling environment for mediation is essential to the success of the process. This requires careful choice of location, skillful mediation, confidentiality, disposition of the parties and appropriate physical arrangement. When all these elements are aligned, the environment is set for constructive communication, mutual understanding and the search for solutions that reflect the interests and needs of the parties involved.

- How to prepare the parties involved for the mediation session

Preparing the parties involved for a mediation session is a crucial step in ensuring the process is productive and effective. This preparation covers several aspects, from mindset to gathering relevant information.

First, it is essential that the parties understand the purpose of mediation. They must understand that the goal is to seek collaborative solutions and find common ground that meets their interests and needs. This requires a mindset of openness, a willingness to listen, and an approach that seeks mutual understanding rather than litigation.

In addition, parties must be willing to share relevant information. This includes details about the conflict, your concerns, goals, and any other points that may be pertinent to resolution. The more information the mediator has, the better he can facilitate the process.

Preparation also involves identifying the main points to be discussed. Parties should consider what topics are most important to them and what they want to achieve through mediation. Having a clear idea of your own goals will help guide the discussion and keep you focused.

It is important to remember that mediation is an opportunity for parties to express their perspectives. They must be willing to listen actively, respect the opinions of others, and consider different points of view. Empathy is a valuable tool here, allowing parties to understand each other's concerns and interests.

Finally, the parties must be willing to work together to find solutions. This may involve giving in on certain points to reach a mutually acceptable agreement. A collaborative mindset is essential, and parties must be willing to compromise to achieve a positive outcome.

Preparing the parties involved for the mediation session is a vital part of the process. It requires an open mindset, willingness to share information, identifying talking points, empathy, active listening and a collaborative approach. When the parties are adequately prepared, the mediation session is more likely to be productive and lead to a constructive resolution of the conflict.

Chapter 4: Mediation Techniques

In the fourth chapter, we will enter the world of mediation techniques, a set of valuable tools that enable the mediator to guide the parties towards collaborative solutions. These techniques are essential for helping parties explore interests, communicate effectively, and find common ground.

A key technique is active listening. The mediator must listen not only to the words, but also to the underlying emotions and interests of each party. This makes it possible to understand the motivations of both sides, helping to identify points of agreement and resolve differences.

Asking questions is another valuable skill. The mediator asks open-ended questions that encourage the parties to explore their points of view and goals. These questions are designed to deepen understanding, surface relevant information, and help parties consider different perspectives.

Time management is a crucial technique. The facilitator must keep the process moving, ensuring that each point is discussed effectively and that the session does not stray or drag on too long. Maintaining a balance between thorough exploration of topics and focus is key.

Furthermore, reframing is a powerful technique. The mediator summarizes what he heard, allowing the parties to verify that their perspective was understood correctly. This promotes clarity and prevents misunderstandings, ensuring everyone is on the same page.

Creativity is a skill that the mediator must cultivate. He can suggest creative solutions that meet the interests of both parties. These "out of the box" solutions often open up new possibilities and help overcome impasses.

Finally, mediation also involves facilitation techniques. The mediator helps the parties find their own solution by providing support, structure and facilitating communication. This allows the parties to work together to reach a mutually acceptable agreement.

These mediation techniques are essential to the success of the process. They enable the mediator to guide the parties through the complexities of the conflict, explore interests and needs, overcome obstacles and, ultimately, reach solutions that reflect the goals and interests of all involved.

- Most common mediation approaches and models

In the world of mediation, different approaches and models are used to adapt to the specific needs of different types of conflicts.

Each approach has its own distinct characteristics and techniques, allowing the mediator to choose the best strategy based on the context of the conflict and the parties involved.

One of the most well-known approaches is the so-called "facilitative approach". In this model, the mediator acts as an impartial facilitator, helping the parties to explore their interests, needs, and concerns. The mediator asks open-ended questions, encourages dialogue, and helps the parties reach their own solutions. This approach is particularly suited to conflicts where the preservation of the relationship is important, such as family issues or business disputes.

Another approach is the "evaluative approach". Here, the mediator plays a more active role, offering assessments and suggested solutions based on their experience and knowledge. This is useful when parties are at an impasse or when they need technical guidance. The evaluative approach is often used in legal disputes or in situations where technical issues are relevant.

A third approach is the "narrative approach". In this model, the mediator helps the parties tell their stories, exploring how they got to their current situation and what their future aspirations are. This approach is especially valuable in conflicts where mutual understanding is essential and when the parties have an emotional connection to the dispute.

In addition to these approaches, several specific mediation models are also applied, such as transformative mediation, community mediation, online mediation, among others. Each of these models has its own guidelines and principles that align with different contexts and objectives.

Understanding these approaches and models is crucial for the mediator to choose the most appropriate strategy for the parties involved and for the type of conflict in question. This allows for more effective mediation, tailored to the specific needs of the parties and the nature of the dispute.

- Facilitation techniques and active listening of the mediator

Facilitation techniques and active listening are two key skills a skilled mediator must master to conduct an effective mediation. These techniques are fundamental to create an environment conducive to communication, mutual understanding and the construction of collaborative solutions.

Facilitation involves directing the mediation process in a constructive way. The mediator plays an impartial guiding role, ensuring that the discussion moves forward in a productive manner. It does this by encouraging equal participation by the parties, establishing clear rules of communication, and focusing on the goals of the mediation.

In addition, the mediator must be able to adapt his approach according to the needs of the parties and the dynamics of the conflict. This might involve changing the pace of the conversation, reframing questions, or introducing specific techniques for overcoming obstacles.

Active listening is an essential technique the mediator uses to fully understand each party's perspectives and concerns. This means listening not only to the words, but also to the underlying emotions, subtext, and interests. The facilitator demonstrates his attention by asking clarifying questions and restating what he heard to ensure he understood correctly.

Empathy is an integral part of active listening. The mediator must demonstrate a genuine interest in the concerns and perspectives of the parties, acknowledging their emotions and showing that their voices are valued.

The active listening technique also involves managing emotions. The mediator must be able to deal with emotional conflicts, keeping calm and helping the parties to express their feelings constructively, rather than inflaming tensions.

Facilitation techniques and active listening are fundamental pillars of the mediator's work. These skills allow the mediator to create a respectful communication environment, encourage mutual understanding, and help the parties collaborate in finding solutions that meet their interests and needs.

- Strategies for dealing with challenging situations during mediation

Challenging situations can arise during mediation, testing the mediator's ability to keep the process productive and respectful. It is crucial that the mediator is prepared to deal with these challenges, maintaining neutrality, impartiality and the ability to manage the dynamics of the conversation.

An effective strategy is conflict management. The mediator should be alert to signs of tension and, when necessary, step in to keep the discussion on a respectful note. This may involve steering the parties toward common interests, reframing statements to avoid confrontation, and creating a safe space where emotions can be constructively expressed.

In addition, the mediator must be prepared to deal with impasses. When the parties are unable to reach an agreement, the mediator can introduce creative problem solving techniques, encouraging the generation of alternative solutions. These techniques might include brainstorming, provocative questions, or exploring options that serve both parties' interests.

Another important strategy is time management. The mediator must keep the process moving, preventing the discussion from being excessively extended on topics that do not lead to an agreement. This involves identifying when a discussion has reached a stagnation point and steering the conversation towards more relevant issues.

When emotions run high, empathy and validation are essential. The mediator must demonstrate understanding for the concerns and feelings of the parties, recognizing the importance of these emotions. This helps calm tempers and create an environment where the parties feel heard.

Finally, in extreme situations, the mediator may consider holding one-on-one sessions with each party to understand their deeper concerns and to work through the issues more privately. This can help break deadlocks and allow parties to express themselves more openly.

Strategies for dealing with challenging situations during mediation require a combination of communication, conflict resolution and time management skills. A skilled mediator is able to adapt his approach according to the context, keeping the focus on the ultimate goal of seeking solutions that meet the interests and needs of the parties involved.

Chapter 5: Applied Case Study

In the fifth chapter, we will explore an applied case study to illustrate the practical application of the concepts and techniques discussed throughout this e-book. This case study will give us a realistic glimpse of how mediation can be effectively used to resolve a conflict.

Let's imagine a scenario in a work environment, where two employees of a company, João and Maria, have been facing a constant conflict that negatively affects the team and productivity. The mediator in this case will be tasked with facilitating a mediation session to help Hansel and Gretel overcome their differences and work together more harmoniously.

The mediator begins the session by establishing an environment of trust and respect. He explains the mediation process, noting that its objective is to understand the concerns and interests of both parties in order to find solutions that suit both parties.

Next, the facilitator uses active listening techniques to allow Hansel and Gretel to express their perspectives. He asks questions that encourage them to share their feelings about the situation, identify specific concerns, and explore possible reasons for the conflict.

The mediator realizes that there is an issue of inadequate communication between them. Maria feels that João does not include her in team decisions, while João believes that Maria does not recognize her contributions. The mediator uses reframing techniques to help them understand each other's perceptions, clearing up misunderstandings and creating a space for mutual understanding.

Now, the moderator guides the discussion towards identifying solutions. He encourages Hansel and Gretel to explore ways to improve communication and collaboration. They begin to discuss options such as regular meetings to share information, work together on specific projects, and express mutual appreciation for their contributions.

The mediator helps them evaluate the different options, considering the pros and cons of each. Gradually, they begin to see that there are areas of agreement and that they both share a desire to improve the team dynamic.

The mediation session concludes with an agreement. John and Mary agree to implement the discussed solutions, committing to communicate more openly and to recognize each other's contributions.

This applied case study allows us to see mediation in action, showing how a skilled mediator can help parties overcome their differences, build mutual understanding, and arrive at solutions that meet their interests and the needs of the team. It is a clear example of how mediation can be a valuable tool for constructively resolving conflicts in a variety of contexts.

- Analysis of real mediation cases and their outcomes

Analyzing real cases of mediation gives us valuable insights into how this approach can be effective in resolving real-world disputes. We will examine two cases, each with a different outcome, highlighting the lessons we can learn from them.

In the first case, we have a conflict between two neighbors, Ana and Carlos, who are constantly arguing about property boundaries and noise issues. Both were exasperated and communication between them was almost non-existent. The mediator started by establishing an environment of trust and impartiality, allowing Ana and Carlos to share their perspectives.

As the mediation progressed, the mediator used active listening techniques to understand both parties' concerns. It was clear that Ana was concerned about her privacy and felt that the excessive noise was disturbing her daily life. On the other hand, Carlos was concerned about the unauthorized expansion of Ana's fence, which, according to him, was encroaching on his property.

The mediator encouraged them to explore options and consider the impact of their actions on each other. They finally agreed to redesign the fence so that it was within the correct boundaries and set specific times for activities that might cause excessive noise.

The outcome was positive; Ana and Carlos reached an agreement that addressed their concerns and preserved harmony in their neighborhood. Mediation helped them better understand each other's concerns, find common ground, and create solutions that considered both of their interests.

In the second case, we have a dispute in a business context between two companies, where the terms of a contract were not being fulfilled. The mediation started with both parties very rigid in their positions and with a clear lack of mutual trust.

The mediator applied conflict management strategies to smooth out initial tensions. He helped the parties explore each company's underlying goals, identifying concerns with deadlines and quality of delivered products.

However, despite the mediator's efforts, the parties were unable to reach an agreement during the mediation session. The outcome in this case was that the parties chose to proceed with legal proceedings.

This case illustrates that mediation does not always result in an agreement, yet it can help to clarify the concerns and objectives of the parties, who may later reassess their positions and seek other avenues for resolution.

These real cases of mediation highlight the importance of communication, mutual understanding and commitment in the search for constructive solutions. They demonstrate that mediation can be an effective tool for resolving conflicts, but they also recognize that it is not always possible to reach an agreement, and in these cases, mediation can still pave the way for an alternative resolution.

- Exploration of techniques applied in specific cases

Exploring the techniques applied in specific cases allows us to understand how these practical approaches can play a key role in conflict resolution. Let's look at two specific techniques, one applied in the context of a family conflict and another in a business dispute.

In the first case, we have a family dispute between a couple, Luis and Marta, who are facing difficulties regarding the division of property after the divorce. The mediator, rather than focusing directly on the division of assets, used the technique of "reframing" to allow Luis and Marta to share their perspectives and concerns.

The moderator started with open-ended questions, encouraging Luis and Marta to explain why certain assets were important to them. This allowed the underlying emotions to be expressed, and the mediator used the reframing to summarize what he heard, validating the concerns of both.

As the discussion progressed, the facilitator introduced the "interest exploration" technique to help Luis and Marta identify what was really valuable to each other. They realized that owning certain goods had more to do with emotional value than monetary value.

Finally, the mediator applied the "option generation" technique so that Luis and Marta proposed alternative solutions for the division of assets. They ended up agreeing to do a split based on items of emotional value, rather than a purely financial split.

This case exemplifies how reframing, interest exploration, and option generation techniques can be applied in a familiar context, allowing parties to find solutions that address underlying interests and preserve relationships.

In the second case, we have a dispute between two companies, where one accuses the other of violating intellectual property. The mediator used the technique of "identifying common interests" to find common ground between the companies.

The mediator began by exploring the underlying motivations of both parties. It was clear that both companies were concerned about protecting their innovations and maintaining an image of integrity in the marketplace.

The mediator applied the technique of "creating options" to help companies identify ways to collaborate rather than litigate. They discussed the possibility of a joint research partnership that could benefit both parties while preserving their interests in innovation and brand image.

This case illustrates how identifying common interests and creating options can be applied in a business context to turn a conflict into an opportunity for collaboration.

The exploration of these techniques applied in specific cases reveals the power of mediation in finding solutions that go beyond initial positions, meeting underlying interests and preserving relationships, whether in family conflicts or business disputes.

- Lessons learned and insights to enhance mediation skills

Lessons learned from analyzing real cases and exploring mediation techniques are invaluable in improving our skills as mediators. They provide us with valuable insights into how to navigate complex conflicts and achieve constructive outcomes.

A crucial lesson is the importance of active listening. The ability to listen beyond the words and pick up underlying emotions is critical to understanding the parties' real concerns. Active listening creates an environment of trust, allowing parties to feel valued and, in turn, more likely to collaborate in finding solutions.

Another lesson is flexibility. Every conflict is unique, and there is no one-size-fits-all approach. The mediator needs to adapt his techniques to the specific circumstances and personalities of the parties involved. Flexibility also involves being willing to change direction when one approach isn't working, trying different techniques to move forward.

Empathy is a fundamental quality of the mediator. The ability to put yourself in the parties' shoes, understand their concerns, and show respect for their perspectives is essential to building trust. Empathy not only facilitates communication, but also helps create solutions that take into account the genuine interests of all parties.

Furthermore, conflict management is a valuable skill that a mediator must master. Conflicts can generate tensions and heated emotions, and the mediator must be prepared to deal with these situations in a diplomatic way. This involves intervening when necessary to keep the discussion on a constructive note and help the parties overcome impasses.

Self-awareness is also crucial. The mediator must be aware of his own predispositions, prejudices and emotional reactions to avoid unduly influencing the process. Ongoing self-assessment is essential to ensure that the mediator is maintaining neutrality and focusing on the best interests of the parties involved.

Lessons learned from analyzing real cases and applying mediation techniques provide a solid foundation for improving our mediation skills. They remind us of the importance of active listening, flexibility, empathy, conflict management and self-awareness. As we incorporate these lessons into our practice, we become more effective mediators, able to guide parties towards solutions that meet their interests and the needs of the moment.

Chapter 6: Tips and Tricks for Mediators

In the sixth chapter, we'll explore a number of valuable tips and tricks that mediators can apply to hone their skills and maximize the success of mediation sessions. These practical guidelines are based on experience and best practices, offering valuable insights for facilitators of all experience levels.

1. **Sound Preparation**: Prior to each mediation session, take time to understand the context of the conflict, the parties involved, and any underlying issues. The better informed you are, the more effective your role as a mediator will be.

2. **Neutrality and Impartiality**: Remain impartial and neutral throughout the process. Be an objective facilitator, avoiding taking sides or showing preferences for any party involved. This helps build trust and allows the parties to see you as a trusted mediator.

3. **Nonjudgmental Empathy**: Empathize with the parties' concerns and emotions, even if you don't agree with them. Listen carefully and validate the emotions that emerge, creating a safe environment where the parties feel free to express themselves.

4. **Focus on Interests**: Help parties identify their underlying interests rather than sticking rigidly to their starting positions. Exploring interests often reveals areas of agreement and creates space for mutually beneficial solutions.

5. **Skillful Time Management**: Keep efficient track of time during sessions. Prevent the discussion from dragging on irrelevant details and direct the conversation to the core issues. Time management keeps the process moving and allows you to address all necessary issues.

6. **Clarification of Agreements**: At the end of each session, clarify the agreements reached. Make sure the parties clearly understand the proposed solutions and what is expected of them. This avoids later misunderstandings and helps ensure that the agreement is effectively implemented.

7. **Continuous Learning**: Be open to continuous learning. Mediation is a skill that can always be improved. Be willing to reflect on your sessions, seek feedback and learn from other facilitators to become increasingly effective in your practice.

8. **Maintaining Confidentiality**: Respect the confidentiality of information shared during mediation. This is essential to building the parties' trust and creating an environment where they feel comfortable discussing their concerns openly.

These tips and tricks are invaluable tools for mediators looking to improve their skills and ensure that mediation sessions are productive, respectful and successful. By applying these guidelines in your practice, you will be prepared to address a wide range of conflicts and help parties find solutions that meet their interests and needs.

-   Practical guidelines to improve performance as a mediator

The following practical guidelines are valuable for improving your skills as a mediator, ensuring that you can conduct mediation sessions effectively, sensitively and respectfully:

1. In-depth Preparation: Prior to each mediation session, take time to study the case, understand the parties involved, and be aware of the context of the conflict. The more prepared you are, the more confidence you will convey to the parties and the more effective you will be in conducting the process.

two. Sincere Empathy: Cultivate genuine empathy for the concerns and emotions of the parties. By demonstrating that you understand and value their perspectives, you create an environment where parties feel heard and respected, which is critical to a successful mediation process.

3. Neutrality and Impartiality: Remain impartial throughout the entire process. Do not take sides, do not show preferences and avoid influencing the final result. Your neutrality is critical for the parties to trust you as a fair and objective facilitator.

4. Focus on Interests: Direct the parties' attention to their interests rather than their starting positions. Helping them to identify what is really important to them creates opportunities for creative solutions that work for both parties.

5. Active Listening and Communication Skills: Improve your active listening skills. Listen not just to the words, but also to the underlying emotions and subtext. Use effective communication techniques to rephrase, ask open-ended questions, and foster constructive dialogue.

6. Adaptive Flexibility: Recognize that each case is unique. Be willing to adjust your approach according to the dynamics of the conflict, the personalities of the parties, and the specific challenges that arise. Flexibility allows you to adapt to the needs of each situation.

7. Conflict Management: Be prepared to deal with emotional conflicts. Keep calm, direct the discussion when necessary, and help the parties overcome impasses. Your ability to manage conflict is critical to keeping the process moving toward constructive solutions.

8. Effective Closing: At the end of each session, ensure that the parties clearly understand the agreements reached. Be ready to document these agreements accurately and confidentially.

9. Continuous Learning: Be willing to learn from each mediation experience. Seek feedback from parties and other mediators, attend workshops, and continue to develop your skills over time.

10. Business Ethics: Maintain high ethical standards. Respect the confidentiality of shared information, avoid conflicts of interest and always seek to act ethically and responsibly.

By following these guidelines, you will be strengthening your role as a mediator, contributing to a more effective mediation process and helping the parties to find solutions that promote constructive conflict resolution.

- How to gain the trust of the parties involved

Gaining the trust of the parties involved is essential to the success of a mediation. This creates an environment conducive to open communication, exploring solutions and building mutually agreeable agreements. Here are strategies that, when applied effectively, help establish that foundational trust:

1. Neutrality and Impartiality: Be impartial and neutral from the start. The parties must realize that you are not favoritism and are committed to facilitating the mediation process fairly.

two. Empathetic Listening: Demonstrate empathetic and attentive listening. Be genuinely interested in each party's concerns and perspectives. It shows that you value what they have to say and that they are being listened to.

3. Respect and Validation: Show respect for all parties, regardless of their positions. Recognize the validity of your worries and emotions, even if you don't agree with them. This creates an environment where the parties feel respected and understood.

4. Transparency: Be transparent about the mediation process, its objectives and the confidentiality that will be maintained. This helps build trust by letting parties know what to expect and that their information will be handled with care.

5. Communication Skills: Communicate clearly and respectfully. Avoid technical language or complex jargon, and be willing to clarify points whenever necessary. Parties rely on mediators who can convey information in an accessible manner.

6. Flexibility and Adaptation: Show flexibility by adapting your approach to the needs and dynamics of the parties. Be willing to make adjustments when appropriate, demonstrating that you are committed to finding solutions that work for everyone.

7. Process Commitment: Show that you are committed to a fair and balanced process. Don't be in a hurry to reach an agreement, and be willing to allow the parties to voice their concerns before starting to explore solutions.

8. Professional Competence: Show that you have the necessary skills and knowledge to guide the mediation process. This builds confidence in the parties knowing they are under the guidance of a competent mediator.

9. Confidentiality: Strictly maintain the confidentiality of information shared during mediation. This is crucial to creating a safe environment where parties can discuss sensitive issues without fear of disclosure.

10. Empathy and Integrity: Demonstrate empathy for the parties and practice mediation with integrity. Be honest, ethical and seek the best outcome for all parties involved.

Gaining the trust of parties requires a careful balance between empathy, neutrality, competence, and respect. By demonstrating these qualities, you will establish the trust necessary for the parties to feel comfortable engaging in the mediation process, making it more effective in finding constructive solutions to the conflict.

- Tactics for conducting mediation impartially and effectively

Conducting a mediation impartially and effectively is an art that requires sensitivity, interpersonal skills and a deep understanding of the principles of mediation. Here are some key tactics you can employ to achieve that goal:

1. Balanced Approach: From the beginning of the mediation, be neutral and impartial. That means not taking sides, not showing preferences, and not letting your own opinions influence the process.

two. Non-Verbal Communication: Be aware of your body language, facial expressions and tone of voice. Maintain a neutral and attentive posture, demonstrating that you are listening and respecting each party equally.

3. Active Listening: The ability to listen carefully is critical. Allow each party to express their concerns and perspectives without interrupting them. This not only validates your emotions, but also helps you to understand the conflict in depth.

4. Rephrase and Clarification: Use rephrase to summarize what you heard, ensuring parts feel understood. When necessary, ask clarifying questions to ensure you have a complete understanding of what is being communicated.

5. Focus on Interests: Refocus parties on identifying their underlying interests rather than their starting positions. Help them explore why certain aspects are important to them, seeking to find areas of convergence and solutions that meet these interests.

6. Session Control: Maintain control of the mediation session in a neutral and impartial manner. Prevent one party from dominating the conversation or the conflict from becoming overly emotional. Keep the focus on the core issues and steer the discussion towards constructive solutions.

7. Avoid Judgment: Do not judge the parties or their actions. Show respect for their perspectives, even if you disagree with them. Impartiality is key to creating an environment where parties feel that their concerns are valid.

8. Encourage Cooperation: Encourage collaboration between parties. Show that you believe that together they can find better solutions than adversarial litigation. This encourages a problem-solving rather than confrontational mindset.

9. Adapt to Needs: Recognize that each conflict is unique. Be prepared to adjust your approach according to the dynamics of the case, always maintaining your impartiality.

10. Maintain Confidentiality: Ensure that information shared during mediation is treated with strict confidentiality. This is essential to building trust between the parties and promoting frank discussion.

By employing these tactics skillfully and sensitively, you can conduct mediation impartially and effectively, allowing the parties to feel confident in their ability to facilitate a constructive dispute resolution process.

Chapter 7: Perceptions about Mediation

The seventh chapter invites us to explore deep insights into mediation. It is an opportunity to reflect on the essence of mediation, its implications and the impact that this approach can have on different aspects of life.

Mediation, as we have seen, transcends mere conflicts, becoming a tool of transformation. It is an art that, when mastered, allows the convergence of diverse perspectives and the creation of solutions that transcend initial positions. Its true strength lies in its ability to humanize dispute resolution processes.

As we explored mediation in depth, we realized that it promotes core values such as empathy, respect, mutual understanding and collaboration. These values are pillars of healthy societies and close-knit communities. Mediation is not just a technique, but a catalyst for building more harmonious relationships.

Perceptions about mediation also reveal its relevance in different contexts. Whether in the family sphere, where it can preserve cohesion between loved ones, or in business, where it can save commercial relationships and avoid costly litigation, mediation extends its wings in many domains.

This approach inspires us to see conflicts not as insurmountable obstacles, but as opportunities for growth and innovation. We realize that, in a world filled with differences and disagreements, mediation is a guiding light to peaceful resolution.

To understand mediation is to embrace a humanistic and practical approach. It is recognizing that all of us, at some point, may find ourselves involved in conflict and that mediation offers a path of hope and understanding.

Therefore, as you conclude this chapter, it is crucial to carry with you the realization that mediation is more than a technique – it is a philosophy of harmony and understanding, a powerful tool that, when applied with sensitivity and skill, can truly transform the way you live. we deal with our disagreements, building a more collaborative and compassionate world.

- Experiences and reports of experienced mediators

Exploring the experiences and accounts of experienced mediators is a fascinating way to delve into the world of mediation, delving into the stories that have shaped the understanding and practice of this art. Allow me to share some of these stories that offer valuable insights:

There was a veteran mediator who shared an inspiring experience in divorce mediation. The parties were in an intense conflict, filled with resentments and hurt accumulated over the years. The mediator realized that, in order to move forward, it was necessary for the parties to feel heard and validated.

Sensitively, the mediator created an environment where each party could express their emotions without being interrupted. They shared their perspectives, the reasons they were hurt, and the impact the divorce had on their lives and families. The mediator not only listened, but reframed these emotions, validating the feelings of both parties.

As the discussion progressed, a surprising thing happened: the parties began to notice shared emotions. Mutual validation defused the tension, allowing them to see that they were both hurting in different ways, but still shared common ground of pain.

With that realization, the parties were open to exploring solutions that had not been considered before. They recognized that divorce was inevitable, but they wanted to ensure that it affected their children's lives and their own emotional health as little as possible. The mediator helped them create a detailed agreement that addressed these concerns, resulting in a less contentious divorce and a plan that benefited everyone.

This account illustrates how an experienced mediator can create a safe and empathetic environment, allowing parties to share their emotions and perspectives, opening doors to creative solutions. This mediator's experience reflects how mediation goes beyond mere legal agreements, providing space for healing and mutual respect.

Another captivating story is of a mediator who handled a commercial dispute between two companies. The conflict involved intellectual property issues and was quickly turning into a costly court battle.

The mediator saw that both companies were firmly rooted in their positions and that the litigation was undermining not only their finances but also their reputation in the marketplace. The mediator used the technique of "identifying common interests", helping the companies to realize that, deep down, they both wanted to protect their innovations and maintain an image of integrity.

On that basis, the facilitator conducted a creative "option generation" session. The companies explored the possibility of collaborating on research and development, a path that would not only resolve the conflict but also bring mutual benefits.

The parties, initially skeptical, ended up embracing this idea. The mediator assisted in crafting an agreement that outlined the terms of this collaboration, protecting both parties' innovations and allowing them to work together on a joint project.

This story underscores the experienced mediator's ability to identify common interests and stimulate creativity to turn a conflict into an opportunity for collaboration. This not only saved the companies money and time, but also created a more constructive relationship between them.

These experiences shared by experienced mediators show us that mediation is a powerful tool that goes beyond conflict resolution; it is a means of human connection, transforming adversity into opportunity and building solutions that reflect the genuine interests of all parties involved. These stories underscore the mediator's vital role in guiding this process, demonstrating how a skillful and sensitive approach can create remarkable results.

- Reflections on the challenges and rewards of mediation

To reflect on the challenges and rewards of mediation is to delve into the deep waters of human complexity, where conflicts arise and opportunities for transformation flourish. Mediation, as with any significant human endeavor, carries with it a number of challenges, but it also offers rewards that transcend the immediate.
Challenges:
1. **Intense Emotions**: One of the main challenges is dealing with the intense emotions that are often present in conflict situations. Stakeholders can bring anger, frustration and resentment, which can create an emotionally charged environment.
2. **Impasses**: Mediation can sometimes encounter impasses, where the parties cannot reach an agreement. Overcoming these moments requires creativity and patience, as well as conflict management skills.
3. **External Pressure**: Mediators may face external pressures such as deadlines, party expectations and legal complexities. The ability to remain focused and effective under these pressures is crucial.

4. **Challenging Communication**: Parties to a conflict are not always able to communicate constructively. The mediator must navigate this dynamic and foster effective communication, ensuring both parties' voices are heard.

5. **Complexity of Issues**: Some conflicts involve complex issues, such as legal or technical disputes, that require a thorough understanding. The mediator may need to gain knowledge about these areas to facilitate an effective process.

Rewards:

1. **Positive Transformation**: The greatest reward of mediation is the ability to facilitate positive transformation in conflicts. Seeing the parties reach mutually agreeable agreements and realizing the relief it brings is deeply rewarding.

2. **Preservation of Relationships**: Mediation often preserves or enhances relationships that might otherwise be irreparably damaged by litigation. This can be especially significant in cases involving families or businesses.

3. **Personal Satisfaction**: Mediators report a sense of accomplishment knowing they are making a difference in people's lives by helping them find solutions that align with their interests.

4. **Creativity and Innovation**: The search for creative solutions is an intrinsic part of mediation. Finding innovative ways to approach problems and create personalized agreements is intellectually stimulating.

5. **Constant Learning**: Each mediation brings learning. Mediators are constantly evolving, improving their communication skills, conflict management and understanding of human complexities.

Ultimately, mediation is a journey of challenges met with skill, empathy and perseverance, with rewards that transcend the immediate process, positively impacting the lives of the parties involved and enriching the mediator's own journey. It's a delicate balance, where challenges are turned into opportunities for growth and rewards resonate beyond the mediation rooms, leaving a legacy of constructive conflict resolution.

- How mediation can transform relationships and communities

Mediation is a transformative force that goes beyond resolving individual disputes. Its impact reverberates in the relationships between the parties involved and transcends to the wider communities, leaving a legacy of understanding, collaboration and harmony.

First, mediation transforms the relationships between the parties themselves. When people find a space where they can voice their concerns, be genuinely heard, and contribute to finding solutions, something profound happens. Not only does this resolve the immediate conflict, but it often rebuilds trust and paves the way for healthier future interactions.

In family situations, mediation can bring together members who have grown apart, such as couples facing amicable divorces who want to continue co-parenting effectively, or families who want to overcome inheritance conflicts. In these circumstances, mediation not only resolves legal issues, but strengthens the emotional foundation of these relationships.

Furthermore, mediation has a profound impact on communities. A clear example is its application in school conflicts, where it can prevent bullying and build a safer educational environment. By dealing with conflict from an early age, children learn to solve problems in a healthy way, a skill they will carry with them into adulthood.

In companies, mediation can reverse the erosion of trust between employees, creating a more productive and collaborative environment. Fosters a culture of conflict resolution that values dialogue over litigation, driving efficiency and job satisfaction.

In the wider community, mediation fosters a culture of respect, empathy and dialogue. It can be used to address complex social issues such as neighborhood disputes, intercultural tensions or intergroup conflicts. Mediation creates a space where the interests of all parties can be heard and where constructive solutions can be found, avoiding polarization and promoting social cohesion.

Mediation, by transforming relationships and communities, plays a key role in building a more peaceful and collaborative world. His sensitive approach and his ability to seek solutions beyond the immediate issues remind us of the incredible ability we have to resolve our conflicts in a humane, dignified and constructive way. It's a tool that, in the right hands, cultivates harmonious dispute resolution and paves the way for healthier relationships and more cohesive communities.

Chapter 8: Closing and Continuity

We have reached the last chapter, a moment of closure, but also of continuity. This is where we reflect on the journey of mediation, recognize its importance and look to the future with hope and commitment.

Ending a mediation is more than simply reaching an agreement or making a final decision. It's about recognizing the progress that has been made, the barriers that have been overcome and the solutions that have been created. It is a time to celebrate the power of communication, empathy and constructive conflict resolution.

But closure is not a final goodbye. Mediation leaves a lasting mark on the parties involved. It provides a fresh perspective on how to tackle disputes in the future, an approach that values mutual understanding over confrontation. The knowledge gained during mediation is a tool that parties can use to resolve conflicts more effectively in their lives.

Furthermore, mediation invites us to think beyond the individual case. She reminds us of the power we have to shape relationships and communities through collaborative approaches. Continuity lies in our continued commitment to constructively resolving conflicts, whether as mediators, as parties or as members of a society that values harmony.

As we close this chapter and our exploration of mediation, we take with us not only techniques and skills, but also a deeper understanding of humanity and the importance of listening and understanding. We close with gratitude for the opportunity to participate in this process and with a promise to continue to promote dialogue and collaboration wherever possible.

The future is a space where mediation remains a shining light, an approach that offers hope in the midst of conflict and reminds us that, however complex the challenges, we can find solutions together. May this journey through mediation inspire us to create a more compassionate world, a place where differences are respected, conflicts are resolved constructively, and where communication is the key to peace.

- Closure of mediation and finalization of agreements

The closing of the mediation is a moment of closure, but also of celebration. It is when the parties, together with the mediator, consolidate the efforts and conclusions reached during the process, giving tangible form to the resolution they sought.

At this point, the parties often experience a sense of relief, knowing that they have reached an agreement that satisfies their concerns and interests. The settlement can be about a wide range of issues, from family disputes to complex business disputes. Regardless of the nature of the conflict, closing mediation represents a significant step toward resolution.

The finalized agreement is itself a testament to the power of mediation. It reflects the parties' ability to communicate constructively, to consider each other's interests, and to find common ground that serves both parties. The agreement is the tangible result of a process that fostered empathy, understanding and collaboration.

The importance of closure cannot be underestimated. It brings a sense of closure to conflict, allowing parties to let go of past tensions and move forward. The agreement can be legally binding, providing a solid basis for future actions. This is especially significant when dealing with ongoing relationships, such as co-parenting in divorce cases or continuing business arrangements.

In addition, closing the mediation is an opportunity to recognize the joint efforts of the parties and the mediator. It is a time to celebrate the ability to resolve disputes peacefully and constructively. This experience not only meets the parties' immediate needs, but also nurtures an environment of collaborative resolution that can extend into their personal and professional lives.

Although mediation formally ends in an agreement, its impact transcends that moment. It leaves a lasting mark on the parties involved, inspiring a more compassionate and collaborative approach to future challenges. The end of mediation is therefore also a beginning, a starting point for a more harmonious way of dealing with disagreements, a demonstration that communication can be a bridge, not a barrier.

Therefore, by finalizing the mediation and consolidating the agreement, we remember that we are planting seeds of constructive resolution that can flourish in future interactions, in the communities we inhabit and in the relationships we maintain. It is a closure that fills us with hope for a future where conflicts can be faced with empathy, where collaboration prevails over strife, and where communication is a powerful tool for peace.

- The importance of follow-up after mediation

The importance of post-mediation follow-up is a crucial facet of the process that should not be underestimated. It represents an ongoing link between the initial resolution of a conflict and building healthier relationships, as well as maintaining the established agreement.

After the formal closure of mediation and the finalization of agreements, it is natural for the parties to return to their lives, dealing with the changes that the agreement may have brought. Follow-up is the mechanism that ensures that the agreement works in practice and that the parties are satisfied with the outcome over time.

This follow-up can take place in several ways:
1. Effectiveness Assessment: From time to time, the mediator may contact the parties to assess how the agreement is working in

practice. This allows you to identify any issues that may have arisen and make adjustments if necessary, ensuring that the agreement remains a viable solution for both parties.

two. Ongoing Guidance: The mediator can offer guidance on how to handle potential challenges that may arise as the parties implement the agreement. This might include tips on effective communication, conflict management or problem solving.

3. Flexibility for Changes: Follow-up allows parties to feel supported and confident to make changes to the agreement if circumstances evolve. This is especially important in agreements that affect ever-changing issues, such as co-parenting agreements.

4. Maintaining Relationships: Follow-up reinforces the idea that mediation is not just about resolving an isolated conflict, but about building healthier relationships. By staying in touch, the mediator can help the parties maintain this mindset, strengthening the likelihood of constructive communication in the future.

The importance of follow-up is even more evident in cases involving long-term agreements, such as family resolutions or business contracts. In these situations, the parties may face unforeseen challenges that require adjustments to the original agreement. Follow-up ensures that parties do not feel isolated, but have a foothold to discuss issues that may arise.

Additionally, follow-up is an opportunity to reinforce the effectiveness of mediation as a positive approach to conflict resolution. As parties experience the benefits of a collaboratively reached agreement, they can share their experiences with others, encouraging a culture of peaceful dispute resolution.

Therefore, post-mediation follow-up is an investment in the continued success of settlements, maintaining relationships, and promoting a more constructive approach to dealing with future challenges. It is living proof that mediation is not just a one-off event, but a transformational journey that continues to have a positive impact long after the initial agreement.

- Final thoughts on the art of mediation and its positive impact

Our final considerations on the art of mediation reveal a panorama of profound positive impact. Mediation, as a conflict resolution tool, transcends the mere pragmatic aspect. It is an expression of the human capacity to seek understanding, find collaborative solutions and cultivate harmony.

Along this journey, we explore how mediation combines empathy and effective communication to turn disputes into opportunities for growth. We have seen that this approach not only resolves conflicts, but also preserves relationships, nurtures communities, and strengthens ties between the parties involved.

Mediation is not just a technique, but a philosophy of embracing the complexity of the human condition. She reminds us that even in the most tense moments, there is room for dialogue, for consideration of the other's feelings and concerns. Through mediation, voices that were once in conflict find common ground, and collaboration emerges from contention.

The positive impact of mediation extends beyond the individual case. It reverberates in families, businesses, schools and communities, fostering an environment where constructive conflict resolution is valued. That impact is a lasting gift that mediation offers to all those involved in the process.

The art of mediation is the art of transformation, and all those who engage in it are artists in some sense, carving solutions out of the raw block of disagreement. By working on this art, we shape a more peaceful and compassionate world, where communication is a powerful tool for overcoming challenges.

As we conclude this exploration, we take with us the understanding that mediation is a beacon of hope. It is a tangible way of demonstrating that cooperation can win over conflict, that understanding is possible even in the most difficult situations.

Our final remarks, therefore, are an invitation to embrace this approach, to cultivate the capacity to listen, to value differences and to seek constructive solutions. It is a celebration of the journey that has brought us here, and also a commitment to continue to advance the art of mediation, lighting the way to a future where peace is more than a distant ideal – it is a reality we build together, a resolution conflict that honors our shared humanity.

- Additional resources to deepen your knowledge in mediation

For those who wish to deepen their mediation knowledge, there are a wealth of resources available. Here are some suggestions that span a variety of formats:

1. **Books**:

- "The Mediation Process: Practical Strategies for Resolving Conflict" by Christopher W. Moore: A classic reference that explores the steps of the mediation process and provides practical insights.

- "Getting to Yes: Negotiating Agreement Without Giving In" by Roger Fisher, William Ury, Bruce Patton: While not specifically about mediation, this book is a must-read on negotiation and offers valuable principles for mediators.

2. **Online Courses**:

- Platforms such as Coursera, edX and Udemy offer online courses on mediation. Some courses are taught by experienced professionals in the field.

- Look for courses that offer recognized certifications to increase your credibility as a mediator.

3. **Workshops and Onsite Training**:

- Many organizations specializing in mediation offer face-to-face workshops and training. Look for local or national institutions that offer training opportunities.

4. **Professional Organizations**:

- Join mediation organizations such as the Brazilian Association of Mediation Professionals (ABRAMEDI) or the International Mediation Institute (IMI). These organizations provide resources, events, and networking opportunities.

5. **Conferences and Events**:

- Attend mediation related conferences to meet experts, exchange experiences and learn from the latest trends. The World Mediation Conference (ICWM) is an example.

6. **Blogs e Podcasts**:

- Many mediation professionals share their experiences and knowledge through blogs and podcasts. They can offer practical insights and valuable perspectives.

7. **Mentoring**:

- Seek mentors in the area of mediation. Having an experienced mediator as a mentor can provide valuable guidance and help you develop your skills.

8. **Free Online Resources**:

- There are many free resources available on the internet, including articles, videos and documents on mediation. Take advantage of these resources to deepen your understanding.

Remembering that practice is fundamental to becoming a skilled mediator. By combining theoretical learning with hands-on experience, you will be well on your way to becoming an effective mediator and making a positive contribution to conflict resolution.

- Useful forms and templates for mediation practice

The practice of mediation can benefit from forms and templates that help structure the process, keep accurate records, and ensure that the parties understand the procedures. Here are some useful forms and templates:

1. **Mediation Agreement**: A document that sets out the rules and expectations for mediation, including confidentiality, mediator impartiality, and agreement to participate in good faith.

2. **Consent Form**: A form that the parties sign to confirm that they are willing to participate in the mediation and accept the established rules.

3. **Information Form**: A document that provides detailed information about the mediation process, clarifying the role of the mediator, the objectives of the mediation and the steps involved.

4. **Topics To Be Covered List**: A guide that helps the mediator to address the main topics during the mediation session, ensuring that no important aspects are left out.

5. **Mediation Agreement Template**: A template that can be adapted to reflect the specific terms of the agreement reached by the parties during mediation.

6. **Action Plan Template**: A detailed plan that the parties can create together to implement the agreement after mediation.

7. **Mediation Session Log**: A document that records the points discussed, proposed solutions, and any decisions made during each mediation session.

8. **Post-Mediation Evaluation Questionnaire**: A form to obtain feedback from the parties on the effectiveness of the mediation, the performance of the mediator, and possible areas for improvement.

9. **Legal Forms**: Depending on the legal context in your region, it may be helpful to have standardized forms, such as a legally binding statement of agreement, prepared with the help of a lawyer.

10. **Evaluation Resources**: Templates for assessing party satisfaction after the mediation process has closed, measuring positive impact and identifying opportunities for improvement.

Keep in mind that these forms and templates must be adapted to the specific needs of each mediation case and local regulations. They serve as tools that can increase the effectiveness and organization of the mediation process, providing clear guidance for all parties involved.

- Bibliographic references and research sources

Here are some bibliographical references and research sources that are valuable for those who want to deepen their knowledge in mediation:

1. **Books**:
- Moore, Christopher W. (2014). "The Mediation Process: Practical Strategies for Resolving Conflict".
- Fisher, Roger; Ury, William; Patton, Bruce (2011). "Getting to Yes: Negotiating Agreement Without Giving In".
- Bush, Robert A. Baruch; Folger, Joseph P. (2005). "The Promise of Mediation: The Transformative Approach to Conflict".
- Ury, William (1993). "Getting Past No: Negotiating in Difficult Situations".

2. **Academic Journals and Articles**:

- Harvard Negotiation Law Review: Provides quality articles on negotiation, mediation, and alternative dispute resolution.
- "Mediation Quarterly" published by Wiley: An important resource for mediation research.
- "Negotiation Journal" published by the Harvard Law School Program on Negotiation: Addresses issues of negotiation and conflict resolution, including mediation.

3. **Organizations and Institutions**:
- Brazilian Association of Mediation Professionals (ABRAMEDI): Offers resources, courses and events related to mediation in Brazil.
- International Mediation Institute (IMI): A global organization that promotes standards of excellence in mediation and provides valuable resources.

4. **Conferences**:
- International Conference on Conflict Resolution Education (CRE): Explores practices and research on conflict resolution in education.
- International Conference on Online Dispute Resolution (ODR): Focuses on technology and innovation in online dispute resolution.

5. **Research Platforms**:
- Google Scholar: Excellent for finding academic articles and research related to mediation.
- JSTOR: A database that includes a variety of academic journals in various disciplines, including dispute resolution.

www.ingramcontent.com/pod-product-compliance
Lightning Source LLC
Chambersburg PA
CBHW062303290526
45794CB00006B/2675

* 9 7 9 8 8 5 6 9 0 5 2 5 9 *